THE
BRIGHT
& HOVE INDEPENDENT CAFÉ GUIDE

A.J. EVANS & L.V. PRICE

Vespertine
Press

First published in the UK by Vespertine Press 2011

Copyright © Vespertine Press 2011
Text © A.J. Evans & L.V. Price
Photography © L.V. Price, Eleonora d'Ambrosio &
James Dean White

A catalogue record of this book is available from
the British Library

ISBN 978-0-9566582-1-0

Cover & layout design by L.V. Price

Printed & bound in the UK by Four Corners Print

All rights reserved, which includes the right to reproduce this
book or portions thereof in any form whatsoever without
the prior written permission of the publishers.

Printed on 9 Lives Offset - paper manufactured from
100% recycled fibre

Recycled
Supporting responsible use
of forest resources
FSC
www.fsc.org Cert no. SA-COC-001654-BT
© 1996 forest stewardship council

100%

CONTENTS

INTRODUCTION

For millions of people around the world, the morning would be incomplete without coffee. Whether prepared at home in a cafetière, sipped at a café table whilst reading the paper or rushed from a take-away cup on the way to work, the much needed caffeine pick-me-up provides a welcome interlude in our daily routine. But over time, not content with its mere stimulating effect, our appreciation for coffee becomes more refined. The aroma, the nuances of flavour and the skill behind its preparation begin to take precedent over the simple purpose of kick-starting our day. It is then that we begin to actively seek out places that can live up to our growing expectations - where every cup far exceeds the weak and bitter stimulant we had for so long accepted, though never loved. At this point it is impossible to go back; the coffee house and café become a part of our everyday lives.

Most people have their own idea of what makes a great café. Some are used primarily as work places while there are others whose well situated pavement terraces provide spectator seats for the passing human cabaret. Then there are the lively meeting spots where discussion drowns out the sounds of the espresso machine and a theory or debate is being expounded at every table. Indeed, ever since the first coffee houses opened in London in the mid-seventeenth century, they became renowned as hotbeds of political discussion as well as trading posts that would go on to spawn institutions like the London Stock Exchange. By the eighteenth century coffee houses were dubbed penny universities - so called because, for the entrance fee of a penny, one had access not only to coffee

6

but to the education afforded by newspapers, pamphlets, discussion and gossip. Conversely, throughout history there have always been cafés purposely frequented by the solitary coffee drinkers, those hideaways for people who, as Viennese satirist and café enthusiast Arthur Polgar says, "*want to be alone but need companionship to do so.*"

Whilst the criteria for a great café still has much to do with its situation and ambience, today the merits of its coffee matters more than ever before. Since the advent of the first Gaggia espresso machines in the 1940s, the general standard of coffee and espresso based drinks has risen. Coffee is now often regarded as a speciality foodstuff much like wine and is diligently sampled and produced with the same expert attention. Nowadays, becoming a barista is a career choice rather than just a part-time job and the role of the master taster, who cups and grades coffee on its aromas, flavours, tastes and 'mouthfeel', has become increasingly prevalent. The popularity and appeal of the World Barista Championship, held in London for the first time last year, has also grown extraordinarily since its inception in 2000. The coffee movement today - sometimes referred to as the Third Wave of Coffee - focuses on improving every stage of coffee production, with an insistence on using only speciality grade Arabica beans, promoting single origin coffees from around the world and achieving perfection in latte art. Aside from the greater levels of expertise and quality coffee that is being promoted at present, there is also a greater emphasis being placed on supporting the livelihoods of coffee farmers and with taking a more pragmatic approach to the plight of coffee producing nations. For example, charitable organisations such as Coffee Kids are raising awareness for the plight of coffee growers and have implemented programs in some of the most at risk coffee growing communities to improve health care, education and social livelihoods. The Black Gold Foundation is another recent addition to the growing number of like-minded partnerships, set up in order to inspire debate and change in relation to international trade justice issues. The discussion regarding the merits of Fair Trade in relation to the Direct Trade model is a complex issue but the independent coffee industry leans more towards Direct Trade when sourcing coffee beans; a system of trading that cuts out both the middle men and the organisations who have the ability to control certification. This approach helps the coffee suppliers to deal more closely with the farmers themselves, building mutually beneficial relationships, addressing social and environmental concerns and paying them a price relative to the quality of the coffee they produce.

One of the earliest roasters to follow these principles in the UK was London's Monmouth Coffee, though the trend has been established for some time in nations such as Australia and America, where they have enjoyed a more evolved coffee drinking culture. Unfortunately it has taken far longer for the British to relax their allegiance to the greasy spoons and tea rooms where the standard of coffee is generally low, instead of frequenting independent cafés and becoming more interested in coffee. Whilst it is still seen as a nation developing its coffee drinking habits, in London and the South East - where 75% of our yearly espresso is consumed - speciality coffee roasters and high end cafés have flourished in recent years.

The city of Brighton and Hove has long since possessed all the ingredients necessary for a thriving café culture. The vibrant street markets and shopping areas, its abundance of bars and restaurants whose tables spill over onto the pavements, as well as the eccentric characters, street performers and musicians that fill the city's streets, all go towards the creation of a cosmopolitan and care-free atmosphere. The diverse mix of residents and visitors, a thriving arts scene and its reputation for welcoming a largely liberal, bohemian crowd also contribute to the cafés' popularity here. Now, with the help of café owners and virtuoso baristas from historically strong coffee cultures, as well as the growing diversity of the London scene, the city's profile for high standards of independent cafés and their coffee is finally living up to its other well renowned virtues.

Even a city like Brighton and Hove, which prides itself on its autonomy and support of local trade, is continuing to suffer the effects of recession and of multinational companies squeezing the life from smaller independents. Furthermore, the state of the worldwide economy is affecting independent cafés and coffee shops as, due to poor weather in South America and a rise in demand for green coffee beans, the price of coffee has recently risen to a thirteen year high. Supporting local independent businesses is therefore more pertinent than ever and must continue and improve should they survive in their current number and quality.

Since the publication of the first edition of this book, we have been overwhelmed by the response and the support people have shown for the project. We would like to thank everyone who has helped in the making of these publications and to you, the reader, for taking an interest in Brighton's burgeoning coffee scene. We hope that you frequent and enjoy the independent cafés of Brighton & Hove as much as we do and that in some small way, this book will continue to help showcase and promote the excellence of our independent cafés as well as local businesses throughout the city.

A.J. Evans

NORTH LAINE

Though there is much debate as to its official origins, the term *laine* is thought to be derived from an Anglo Saxon expression meaning smallholding or strip of land and bears no relation to the word lane. In the mid-nineteenth century the area was largely populated by saw-mills and foundries, and home to Brighton's largest slum, but in the last thirty years the North Laine has blossomed into a vibrant, bohemian area regarded by many to be the heart of the city. Some of Brighton's most famous cultural attractions, such as the Royal Pavilion, the Brighton Dome and the Theatre Royal are located within the North Laine. Today, the North Laine is also renowned for its array of second hand and vintage clothes boutiques, specialist book and record shops and its high number of restaurants, bars and largely independent cafés. The laid back bustle of the area is especially enjoyable on the weekends when the Saturday market stalls are set out on Upper Gardner Street and the area is crowded with shoppers and day-trippers making their way to the seafront.

PLACES OF INTEREST

A. Royal Pavilion
B. Brighton Museum & Gallery
C. Dome Theatre
D. Theatre Royal
E. Jubilee Library
(please see map for locations)

TAYLOR ST. BARISTAS

28 Queen's Road, Brighton BN1 3XA
T: 01273 735 466 www.taylor-st.com

Hours - Mon-Fri: 7.30-5.30	Loyalty Card - Yes	Wifi - Yes
Sat: 8 - 5.30	Outdoor Seating - Yes	W.C. - Yes
Sun: 10 - 5	Wheelchair Access - Yes	Alcohol - No

Machine - La Marzocco FB/70	Beans - Union Hand-Roasted
Grinder - Mazzer Robur E & Super Jolly	Soya Milk - Yes

According to the famous proverb, *necessity is the mother of invention,* and It was precisely this notion that led to the creation of Taylor St. Baristas; the brainchild of three Aussie siblings responding to the low standards of coffee on offer in the UK. That the idea arose during a bleak English mid-winter may have led the trio to yearn more acutely for their homeland, though ultimately it wasn't the sunshine that they wished to import to Brighton - it was the coffee.

Five years after their move to the South coast, Taylor St. - named after the road in Sydney where the owners once lived - has remained true to the purpose of its conception. Having outgrown its former base within the confines of the Travelbag shop, the café moved to a much larger site along Queen's Road, near Brighton station. In correspondence with their relocation, Taylor St. has broadened its range of Australian café food to include toasted homemade banana bread, ricotta pancakes and Bircher muesli, along with an extended variety of snacks and sandwiches.

However, striving for coffee perfection is still the main focus at Taylor St. In collaboration with Union Hand-Roasted, their bespoke Rogue espresso blend is designed to promote the diversity and seasonality of coffees from around the world. Throughout the year, as different crops arrive at the roastery, the blend is changed to incorporate and showcase distinctive coffees that are balanced accordingly for variants of flavour. As such, the coffee here is a constant work in progress with the aim of creating a blend for espresso and espresso based drinks, like the flat white or cappuccino, that is sweet, complex and rounded.

Be sure to ask one of the baristas about the current blend components as well as the guest and single origin coffees, available brewed as espresso, AeroPress, filter or pour-over. To ensure that the hard work they put into creating the perfect coffee blend delivers the best possible results, Taylor St.'s baristas are trained in coffee, tea and chocolate theory, equipment use and maintenance, espresso theory and practice, milk texturing and art, alternative brewing methods and tea brewing. Bearing in mind such effort, it's no wonder that Taylor St. are at the vanguard of Brighton's growing coffee scene.

COFFEE@33

33 Trafalgar Street,
Brighton BN1 4ED

Hours - Mon-Fri: 7.30 - 6	Loyalty Card - No	Wifi - No
Sat: 9 - 6	Outdoor Seating - Yes	W.C. - Yes
Sun: 10 - 5	Wheelchair Access - No	Alcohol - No

Machine - La Marzocco Linea	Beans - Monmouth
Grinder - Mazzer Super Jolly	Soya Milk - Yes

Perhaps the greatest charm of a good independent café is its ability to retain the original seeds of spirit that inspired it, without compromising the fundamental elements of quality and service it set out to achieve. Without the need to mass produce or bow down to corporate influence, an independent can nurture the more important elements that go into creating an atmosphere and a standard that its customers can really savour.

A stone's throw from Brighton station, down the busy thoroughfare that is Trafalgar Street, Coffee@33 takes these ideals and pushes them that little bit further. In 2008 the site, which once housed Café Abroad, was stripped back to get to the bare boards and white walls that its new owners sought. The proprietors - a Ukrainian barista and an Italian chef - wanted no distraction from the coffee and food that they ardently create and prepare on site. To this day the décor remains minimal: clean lines, hand-made wooden benches and the coffee sacks used as cushions on the much coveted window seats, all allude in style to the high-end cafés of London.

Using a Monmouth espresso blend of beans from Brazil, Guatemala and Columbia, creates a medium to dark roast with a very smooth finish, one of the many reasons why Coffee@33 are so regularly afforded the 'best coffee in Brighton' tag by locals and visitors alike. Since early 2011, the café has also introduced two single-origin filter options to their coffee menu, both prepared using a Hario V60 coffee dripper. The Gethumbwini Estate from Kenya is a medium roast coffee with a bright acidity and notes of blackberry whilst the Shilcho Cooperative coffee from Ethiopia is full-bodied with dried apricot and nectarine flavours.

Not to be overshadowed, the food is entirely homemade, right down to the lovingly baked focaccia bread. Along with sandwiches and paninis, there are also flapjacks and brownies on offer, and if you're feeling inspired they create cookie dough for you to take away and bake at home.

That cafés like Coffee@33 exist in Brighton is testament to how small scale businesses with the right amount of expertise, zeal and dedication can flourish. This is a place that has been created by coffee and food lovers, *for* coffee and food lovers. In an industry where similar ideals can be overshadowed by the money-driven spectre of big business, Coffee@33 remains happy to be exactly where it is, sticking to what they set out to do in the first place. The beauty of that, like all the best things in life, lies in its simplicity.

MANGE TOUT

81 Trafalgar Street, Brighton BN1 4EB
T: 01273 607 270

Hours - Mon-Wed: 9 - 6	Loyalty Card - Yes	Wifi - Yes
Thu-Sat: 9 - 11	Outdoor Seating - Yes	W.C. - Yes
Sun: 9 - 5	Wheelchair Access - Yes	Alcohol - Yes

Machine - Gaggia Deco	Beans - Small Batch
Grinder - Iberital MC2 Challenge	Soya Milk - Yes

In France it is said that a bistro can become the essence of the neighbourhood in which it dwells, where the routine of its daily life keeps time with the rhythms of its locale. From the early morning coffee, to the lunchtime rush, the afternoon lull and the early evening meal, the café remains a steadfast observer of the passing hours.

On the North side of Trafalgar Street, Mange Tout has more of this relaxed café-bistro feel than most in Brighton, maintaining that traditional Gallic flair for food and drink within a fresh and modern environment. The interior is bright and airy and the south facing windows shed plenty of light onto the morning papers. The blackboard menu wall, the photographic work of local artists and the mixture of modernist and traditional seating all add touches of interest to the surroundings. As a statement of intent, the espresso machine takes pride of place in the café so that the customer can observe a trained barista preparing their coffee, made with Small Batch sourced beans and served the French way - with a glass of water and a miniature meringue.

The terrace of tables and chairs outside is ideal for those who prefer drinking their coffee whilst taking in the passing charms of the avant-garde North Laine crowd. Wherever you decide to position yourself, the food is simple and honest and prepared by highly skilled chefs using wild, organic and free-range produce sourced from local farms and suppliers. The main menu largely consists of French favourites such as moules-frites and, of course, escargot. The tartines and Eggs Benedict, with freshly made Hollandaise sauce, are considered their unofficial speciality and the homemade cakes and pastries are definitely worthy of any self-respecting French kitchen.

Opened in March 2009, the café has already gained a healthy local following. On the weekends, when the North Laine really springs to life, those conversant with Mange Tout's menu flock to sample the fine food, the irrepressible charm of its French owners and the laid back sounds of FIP radio that meander through the café. The union of tradition and modernity infuse Mange Tout with its own unique atmosphere, bringing a contemporary impression of the continental café experience to Brighton. Vive la France!

REDWOOD COFFEE HOUSE

97-99 Trafalgar Street, Brighton BN1 4ER
www.redwoodcoffeehouse.com

NORTH LAINE

Hours - Mon-Fri: 8 - 6	Loyalty Card - Yes	Wifi - Yes
Sat: 10 - 6	Outdoor Seating - No	W.C. - Yes
Sun: 10 - 5	Wheelchair Access - Yes	Alcohol - No

Machine - La Cimbali M22	Beans - Redwood Blend
Grinder - San Remo	Soya Milk - Yes

Opened on the weekend of Pride 2010, Redwood Coffee House may have had to hit the ground running but has quickly found its groove amid the competition for good coffee venues on Trafalgar Street. Inspired by the café culture in Australia and New Zealand, the Antipodean influences are clear - from the ornaments and artwork scattered throughout the ample, two-tiered space, the laid back atmosphere and, most importantly, the coffee. Since its opening, Redwood's baristas have devised their own house espresso blend consisting of coffees from Java, Tanzania and Costa Rica. The breakfast and lunch menus feature giant toasties and grilled ciabattas, alongside breads and pastries, homemade cakes, brownies and flapjacks.

The ample comfy sofa that takes centre stage in the seating area is the perfect spot in which to relax and appreciate everything Redwood offers. The Max Eurmann poem that adorns one of the many chalkboards readily sums up the café's ethos: "Be cheerful, strive to be happy." You'll have every reason to be.

FARM

99 North Road, Brighton BN1 1YE
T: 01273 623 143 www.farmsussex.co.uk

Hours - Mon-Fri: 8.30-4.45	Loyalty Card - No	Wifi - No
Sat: 8.30-4.45	Outdoor Seating - Yes	W.C. - Yes
Sun: 10 - 5	Wheelchair Access - Yes	Alcohol - No

| Machine - CMA Astoria | Beans - Small Batch |
| Grinder - Anfim Milano | Soya Milk - Yes |

Opened in late 2009, Farm is owned and run by a group of local farmers, who grow the vegetables, rear the livestock and produce the dairy products that are used in making the café's homemade meals and sandwiches. This ensures that each of these ingredients have been locally and mindfully produced, that everything has been ethically farmed, is as fresh as possible and remains seasonal throughout the year. Where certain foodstuffs need to be acquired from elsewhere, Farm prides itself in using bread from Ockham's Lighthouse Bakery and coffee from Small Batch.

Inside the café, which is positioned next door to the famous Bill's Produce Store, the feel is unsurprisingly reminiscent of a farmhouse kitchen. The church pews, distressed furniture and milk cans used as stools make the interior a homely, unfussy place in which to relax. Their farmer's market, situated further up North Road, showcases some of the very best local producers selling a whole host of organic and free range wares, bringing yet another slice of the Sussex countryside to the North Laine.

CREAM TEA

13 New Road, Brighton BN1 1UF
T: 01273 325 112

Hours - Mon-Fri: 7 - 6	Loyalty Card - No	Wifi - Yes
Sat: 9 - 6	Outdoor Seating - Yes	W.C. - Yes
Sun: 9 - 6	Wheelchair Access - Yes	Alcohol - No

Machine - Fracino Classic	Beans - Small Batch
Grinder - Fracino Model S	Soya Milk - Yes

As café locations in Brighton go, Cream Tea has a vantage point that is hard to beat. From a seat on their pavement terrace opposite the Pavilion Gardens one can take in the historic charms of Brighton's cultural quarter as well as the sights and sounds of New Road's eclectic street performers and musicians.

Behind its curved glass frontage the café is bright and modern, though with touches of the traditional tea room to which the name refers. The display cabinet at the counter is well stocked with homemade cakes, scones and pastries, with an ice cream machine providing welcome refreshment during the heat of the summer. Along with the customary English Breakfast and Earl Grey tea on offer, the café also serves a selection of loose leaf teas by the renowned Tea Pigs company. Whilst tea rooms are ordinarily not well known for the merits of their coffee, Cream Tea has enlisted the expertise of Small Batch to make sure that their coffee is not only locally sourced and freshly roasted, but also that the standards are up there with the quality of the view.

EAST BRIGHTON
& KEMPTOWN

Kemptown is named after Thomas Read Kemp who formulated the plans for the original Kemp Town estate in the early nineteenth century, creating large and elegant homes for the affluent social elite. Though the one-word title Kemptown now refers to a much larger area, the regency style architecture that is perhaps most notable in the magnificent Sussex Square and Lewes Crescent, still upholds the air of grandeur attributed to the original designs. As a whole, Kemptown is rejuvenated having gained a less than positive reputation in recent years for its generally run down appearance. Today the area is rich in character derived from the originality of its artisan and creative residents, whilst it is also home to a large proportion of Brighton's gay community. Further to the East, the Bristol Estate, Whitehawk and the Craven Hill Estate, are often collectively referred to as East Brighton, whilst to the North and West of Kemptown lies the tranquillity of Queen's Park.

PLACES OF INTEREST

F. Brighton Pier
G. Volks Railway
H. Queen's Park

I. Brighton Racecourse
J. Brighton Marina
(please see map for locations)

GROUND TEA & COFFEE

36 St. Georges Road, Brighton BN2 1ED
T: 01273 696 441   www.groundcoffeehouses.com

Hours - Mon-Fri: 7 - 6	Loyalty Card - Yes	Wifi - Yes
Sat: 8 - 6	Outdoor Seating - Yes	W.C. - Yes
Sun: 8 - 5	Wheelchair Access - Yes	Alcohol - No

| Machine - La Marzocco FB/80 | Beans - Union Hand-Roasted |
| Grinder - Compaq K10 & Mazzer Major | Soya Milk - Yes |

The creation of Ground Tea & Coffee was a labour of love, born out of hard work and expertise that make their recent success all the more gratifying. Aside from accumulating a growing number of loyal followers, Ground scooped the coveted *Best Café* title at Brighton's Foodie Awards ceremony in 2010 and was also amongst the Independent's *Top 50 Cafés* in the UK - and all this in only its first year.

One of the many reasons why Ground has garnered such high praise since opening is that the baristas here serve up consistently great coffee, and are well versed in getting the best from both Union's *Bright Note* blend, used for all their espresso based drinks, and also from the beautiful cherry red La Marzocco machine that occupies the far end of the counter. *Bright Note*, which combines beans from both Guatemalan and Brazilian farms, is of medium body and acidity and has a pronounced fruity tone with notes of vanilla, hazelnut and molasses.

Also on the coffee menu are single estate guest coffees from around the world that are rotated seasonally and are available as filter, AeroPress or as a hand-made pour-over.

As their name suggests, Ground Tea & Coffee also carry a fine selection of loose leaf teas, infusions and herbal tisanes sourced from Jing Teas and the Canton Tea Company, both major names in London. In addition, their breakfast and lunch menus feature locally renowned sandwiches made freshly on site each day, bagels from Brighton's very own Bagelman and delicious croissants, quiches, pastries and cakes from the highly acclaimed Cocoa Patisserie. The attention to detail afforded their drinks and foodstuffs are mirrored in the design of the café itself, with an emphasis on using goods and materials that are ethical and sourced from like-minded businesses.

The south-east facing windows fill the space with light, making for a laid back atmosphere that changes throughout the days and months and there is now even more seating since the addition of a new back room which is also available for private meetings. To round things off, there is a range of good reading material and music that is eclectic and unobtrusive – the perfect accompaniments to any enjoyable café experience.

The components that go into achieving coffee perfection may seem complex, but in fact the message at Ground is simple: if it's not as good as it could be, why bother? It is no accident then, that Ground's results are of such a high quality. Furthermore, 2011 only looks set to further confirm their ascendancy.

REDROASTER
COFFEE HOUSE

1d St. James's Street, Brighton BN2 1RE
T: 01273 686 668 www.redroaster.co.uk

Hours - Mon-Fri: 7 - 7	Loyalty Card - Yes	Wifi - Yes
Sat: 8 - 7	Outdoor Seating - Yes	W.C. - Yes
Sun: 9 - 6.30	Wheelchair Access - Yes	Alcohol - No

| Machine - La Spaziale S3 | Beans - Redroaster |
| Grinder - Mazzer Super Jolly | Soya Milk - Yes |

In the decade since Redroaster established itself on St. James's Street, it has become something of a Brighton institution. From its windows the views of the locality have changed and shifted with the times. The vicinity, once called Little Laine was, even up until several years ago, an area in the midst of slow decline, gaining undesirable monikers that were a far cry from its reputation in the nineteenth century as the Bond Street of Brighton. But whilst the aspect has altered, Redroaster has maintained its immutable appeal, taking root as an integral part of the reinvigorated St. James's street community.

As you would expect from the area, the café attracts a diverse cross-section of visitors which creates a lively, communal atmosphere. Underneath the skylights set into its high ceilings, the sounds of chatter and the aroma of roasted coffee waft throughout the spacious room. The antique coffee grinders on the ledge opposite the counter allude to the home roasting experimentation the café owner undertook when the business was in its fledgling years.

That was during the late eighties and early nineties speciality coffee boom in North America, where US companies were preparing to branch into the European market. It was on this wave of interest that the seeds of Redroaster's influence were sewn in Brighton, setting up shop on the corner of Meeting House Lane and Ship Street in the Lanes. Today, Redroaster has branched out and now run their own separate roastery on Arundel Mews in Kemptown. Here their experts cup, roast and distribute bespoke blends for some of the most established venues in Brighton including Komedia and the Infinity Foods Café. Their head roaster, Paul Stephens, also won the UK Cup Tasting competition held by the Speciality Coffee Association of Europe in 2010.

With its origins so firmly embedded in the creation of fine coffee, it is no wonder that Redroaster's produce has gained such a reputation. As well as boasting an extensive range of single origin coffees from Ethiopia, Peru, India, Brazil and Guatemala, all roasted on site using their eponymous *red roaster*, they also serve sandwiches, flapjacks, pastries and cakes. In the evenings the café becomes home to one-off music events, poetry readings, book launches and even tango lessons.

      With the high turnover of independent cafés in the city, Redroaster's ten year tenure deserves kudos. So whilst sitting under the café's canopy, watching the bustle of St. James's street pass you by, it is worth remembering that times change but quality endures.

FRANKIE'S GRINDER

180 Edward Street, Brighton BN2 0JB
T: 01273 818 888

Hours - Mon-Fri: 7.30-6.30	Loyalty Card - Yes	Wifi - No
Sat: Closed	Outdoor Seating - Yes	W.C. - No
Sun: Closed	Wheelchair Access - Yes	Alcohol - No

Machine - La Marzocco GB/5	Beans - Small Batch
Grinder - Mazzer Super Jolly	Soya Milk - Yes

For the past eight years, Frankie Vaughn's on Edward Street has been lauded by locals as one of the prime lunch spots in Brighton. With a choice range of bespoke sandwiches, bagels and salads, all freshly prepared using mainly local ingredients, perhaps the only attribute missing was a place to sit and enjoy a cup of coffee. But then, in late 2009, Frankie Vaughn's owner set up a boutique coffee bar in the more spacious corner plot next door and kitted it out with a La Marzocco espresso machine, a counter decorated with hessian coffee sacks and all the renowned food options previously confined to their deli. Thus, Frankie's Grinder was born.

To ensure that their coffee lives up to the high standards set by their food, they have designed Little Frankie's Blend with Hove-based coffee roasters Small Batch, which they also sell ready ground to be enjoyed in the comfort of your own home. And if you need your coffee to go, the service hatch that gives onto Prince's Street makes for a speedy return to the office. Lunch breaks have never been so well catered for.

THE LANES

The Lanes, also referred to as the South Lanes, are the heart of the old fishing town of Brighthelmstone. Much of its layout is derived from the paths, or *twitterns*, that once ran between allotments and gardens in the centre of this 14th century dwelling. Today the Lanes are commonly taken to be bounded by the Old Steine to the east and the seafront to the south, along with North Street and West Street - two of the four streets that were marked on the earliest existing map of Brighton. The area is well known as the city's historic centre and is largely populated by antiques and jewellery shops, fashion boutiques, traditional English pubs, restaurants and cafés. Due to their proximity to the seafront, the Lanes are often full of activity, making it the perfect place to window-shop as you meander to the beach. Despite the modernisation of a large proportion of buildings during the 18th and 19th century, the narrow twist of alleyways continue to exude the atmosphere of a medieval town with a number of 400 year-old cottages remaining, as well as the Cricketers, which is claimed to be Brighton's oldest pub.

PLACES OF INTEREST

K. The Lanes Shops

L. Town Hall

M. East Street Shops

N. Quadrophenia Alleyway

O. Fishing Museum

(please see map for locations)

MARWOOD

52 Ship Street, Brighton BN1 1AF
T: 01273 382 063 www.themarwood.com

Hours - Mon-Fri: 8 - 8	Loyalty Card - No	Wifi - Yes
Sat: 10 - 8	Outdoor Seating - Yes	W.C. - Yes
Sun: 10 - 8	Wheelchair Access - Yes	Alcohol - No

| Machine - La Spaziale Special | Beans - Mozzo |
| Grinder - Mazzer Robur E | Soya Milk - Yes |

Ever since the first European coffee house opened in Venice in 1645, great writers, artists and thinkers have used them as unofficial workplaces and meeting spots. Whilst some cafés have become infamous because of their creative inhabitants - think the *Café de Flore* or *Les Deux Magots* in Paris, where Sartre and Simone de Beauvoir founded their existentialist theories - Brighton has never had such a place. That is, perhaps, until now.

Since opening in late 2009, Marwood has rapidly built its reputation amongst the city's large creative community as a place to convene and to work. The very reason Marwood came to fruition was reliant on the work of many such minded people, not just its owner, who all chipped in with their own goods, ideas and services to create a kind of hybrid space of many influences. It is no wonder then that its wonderfully cluttered interior also houses the sense of a community-shared project and is imbued with no small amount of humour.

Manikins adorn the walls alongside framed toy animals and pictures of Tommy Cooper and Michael Jackson, whilst the tables are made from salvaged doors and arranged in such a way that sharing is almost customary, a conscious decision to aid the meeting of new people. New additions to the scenery seem to appear overnight so that the café is forever in a state of eccentric flux. The espresso machine is adorned with fridge magnets, amusing postcards and plastic animal figures, behind which skilled baristas use Mozzo's house blend to create coffees that look almost too good to drink. Though the food menu is limited to snacks like Breville toasties and homemade cakes, the focus on the quality of coffee is enough to warrant a lengthy stay on its own.

Upstairs there is a further seating area known affectionately as the boy's room - a homage to 80's kitsch complete with a record player, an Amstrad computer and Smash Hits posters adorning the walls. The upper stories also accommodate Marwood Studios, which consist of design offices, desk shares and a Mac specialist. And as if there weren't enough to grab your attention, there is also a secret courtyard garden to explore out back – the place to be during the summer months.

Whilst it may be some time before the café becomes famous for any of its clientele, Marwood is nonetheless attracting interest for all the right reasons. As with everything else here, the only rule appears to be that there aren't any...and somehow it seems to be working.

Marwood Studios

Marwood
Coffee Shop

KICK ARSE COFFEE

Life changing CAKE

Open

8am–8pm Weekdays

10am–8pm SAT/SUN

open

CAFÉ COHO

53 Ship Street, Brighton BN1 1AF
T: 01273 747 777

Hours - Mon-Thu: 8 - 8	Loyalty Card - Yes	Wifi - Yes
Fri & Sat: 8 - 10	Outdoor Seating - Yes	W.C. - Yes
Sun: 9 - 5	Wheelchair Access - No	Alcohol - Yes

| Machine - Gaggia Deco | Beans - Union Hand-Roasted |
| Grinder - Anfim Super Caimano | Soya Milk - Yes |

Opened on Ship Street in December 2010, Café Coho is yet another welcome addition to the city's growing number of coffee focused venues. Bearing all the aesthetic hallmarks of a boutique London coffee shop, complete with exposed brick work, stone flooring, rustic wooden benches and industrial-style fixtures, Coho wouldn't look out of place amongst the swathe of new coffee venues that continue to spring up in Soho and Fitzrovia. Continuing its links to the capital, Coho is also the only café in Brighton to use the Revelation Blend from London's Union Hand-Roasted, which is exceptional either when combined with milk – as in a flat white or caffè latte – or as a full bodied espresso shot. In addition, Coho's Australian head barista is certainly well qualified at maximizing the blend, packing 17.5grams of coffee into every shot.

Whether sat at a table on the pavement terrace, perched at the bench seats by the window or upstairs in one of the many armchairs, there are ample vantage points from which to watch the world go by. The cosy nook at the back of the main café also provides that much sought-after quiet spot in which to relax after a long day of shopping or exploring the nearby Lanes.

Alongside the café menu staples of pastries, croissants and sausage rolls, there are also breakfasts, deli-style sandwiches and a range of sweet and savoury snacks, all impeccably displayed upon the counter.

Current favourites on the menu include the pastrami, Dijon mustard, gherkin and rocket pitta bread and the delicious carrot and orange cake. In addition Coho uses local suppliers to source only the best quality seasonal ingredients, including the Real Patisserie and the Home Cakery.

Coho is also available for private hire, where the food takes an up-market turn with carved Spanish ham, Parmesan cheese, rustic breads and chutneys accompanying fine wines, beers and speciality, coffee-based cocktails that flow late into the evening. In many ways Coho is an indication of how Brighton's cafés are borrowing and benefiting from the current coffee explosion in the capital. If these are the results, long may the trade-off continue.

café coho

MORE SEATING UPSTAIRS

COFFEE FROM UNION
HAND ROASTED

CAKES/PASTRIES
LOCALLY MADE

SANDWICHES MADE
DAILY ON PREMISES

WINE / PROSECCO

COOPERS PALE &
SPARKLING ALE

PRIVATE HIRE AVAILABLE

info@cafecoho.co.uk

HOME MADE
SOUP W/BREAD
4.00 IN
3.00 OUT

TIC TOC CAFÉ

53 Meeting House Lane, Brighton BN1 1HB
T: 01273 770 115 www.tictoc-cafe.co.uk

Hours - Mon-Fri: 10 - 6	Loyalty Card - Yes	Wifi - Yes
Sat: 10 - 6	Outdoor Seating - Yes	W.C. - Yes
Sun: 10 - 6	Wheelchair Access - No	Alcohol - No

| Machine - Viva Aurora | Beans - Small Batch |
| Grinder - Fracino Model S | Soya Milk - Yes |

The Lanes of the twenty-first century are densely populated by antiques shops, boutiques and jewellers, but they still retain much of their historical charm. Tucked in the bustling heart of these *twitterns*, housed within a listed building on Meeting House Lane, Tic Toc Café is an ideal place to stop and charge up on caffeine and calories.

The nucleus of the café's design is derived from the coffee shops of Amsterdam, the green of the exterior, for example, being one of only eight shades of colour permitted within the city's famous Jordaan District. But stepping inside it becomes clear that, in both its produce and its décor, Tic Toc draws inspiration from right across Europe. The atmosphere is convivial and homely, akin to that found at a local French bistro or deli, and there is also something distinctly European about borrowing one of the café's blankets and sitting on the small terrace with a cup of Belgian hot chocolate in the winter months.

All this is juxtaposed with sixties-inspired clocks, quirky floral wallpaper, toy ornaments and dashes of historical detail. The mish-mash of antique furniture and feature walls make the interior a space in which one notices a new facet on every visit. The food at Tic Toc is a continuum of its decorative mélange with hearty soups and chunky open sandwiches featuring a large selection of delicious fillings and seasonal variations. There is also a variety of locally made cakes and brownies with which to treat oneself. Furthermore, as runners up in the 2010 Observer Food Monthly Award for *Best Cheap Eats*, the food here is gaining recognition from far and wide.

As with any good cafe the quality of its coffee is paramount, a consideration that Tic Toc's owners addressed early on. Before opening they teamed up with the Small Batch Coffee Company and worked alongside them to create a blend of coffee specific to their own design. The result: a rich taste sweetened ever so slightly by the addition of 4% Indian beans, a combination that goes some way to affirming the cheeky sign outside that reads, *Probablement the best coffee in Brighton*. Certainly, as a place to enjoy some time out, there is no doubt that Tic Toc is one of the city's best.

TIC TOC
CAFÉ
OPEN DAILY
TEL:
01273 770115
www.tictoc-cafe.co.uk

TIC TOC
CAFÉ
OPEN DAILY
TEL:
01273 770115
www.tictoc-cafe.co.uk

PLATEAU

1 Bartholomews, Brighton BN1 1HG
T: 01273 733 085 www.plateaubrighton.co.uk

THE LANES

Hours - Mon-Thu: 9 -11.30	Loyalty Card - No	Wifi - Yes
Fri & Sat: 9 - 12.30	Outdoor Seating - No	W.C. - Yes
Sun: 9 - 12.30	Wheelchair Access - No	Alcohol - Yes

| Machine - La Spazialle S5 | Beans - Small Batch |
| Grinder - Mazzer Super Jolly | Soya Milk - Yes |

Following the success of Mange Tout in 2010, the new year sees the opening of stylish sister venue Plateau. Carrying all the Gallic hallmarks of its counterpart, Plateau nonetheless extends its influences further afield, bringing together elements of world cuisine and the continental café experience to form a fresh new hybrid.

Thanks in no small part to a diligently compiled menu and a head chef with years of experience in various parts of the world, the food options include re-workings on the breakfast menu and an extended selection of main courses, modern tapas and platters, from which the venue garners its name. Expect an elegant French culinary expression but with a unique and global twist. Plateau also has the advantage of a well-stocked bar serving fine spirits, bottled beers, champagne and an extensive wine list featuring mostly organic, natural or biodynamic wines.

Whilst their food focus deserves to take centre stage, the coffee and tea menu at Plateau is not to be outdone. 2011 sees the advent of the new Mange Tout espresso blend, devised by owners Thierry and Vincent alongside Small Batch Coffee Company exclusively for their Brighton venues. Consisting of equal parts Indonesia Tora Toraja and Finca La Candelilla from Costa Rica, the result is a sweet, spiced toffee body and a plummy acidity. Plateau also serves a large selection of speciality teas from the Tea Pigs company.

Situated opposite the grandiose town hall building, Plateau's interior exudes quality; the exposed brickwork, stainless steel counter top, industrial-style furniture, leather benches and tasteful black tiling bring to mind the feel of a modern New York style café. Along with their usual penchant for good music throughout the day, DJs provide the evening entertainment, creating an ambience befitting of the chic surroundings. Add to all this a late license and a highly skilled bar tender and you have all the perfect ingredients to savour, whatever the time of day or night.

WEST BRIGHTON & HOVE

It is said that whereas Hove was built, Brighton grew. It grew until the boundary between them was blurred and until the two combined to form one city. As you head west from Brighton's centre the change occurs gradually with narrow streets and fisherman's houses morphing into the regency splendour of Brunswick Square and Adelaide Crescent, their boulevards lined with trees and parkland. Hove has undoubtedly retained its identity as an independent town with thriving shopping areas and a cultural input that both rivals and complements its larger neighbour.

The western seafront is a many varied strip with old fisherman's arches turned into everything from galleries to nightclubs. The skeleton of the West Pier has changed from derelict eyesore to creative inspiration and the pétanque pitches and Hove's lawns provide both a refuge and a recreation ground. There is certainly much to savour and enjoy in this part of Brighton... and Hove, actually.

PLACES OF INTEREST

P. King Alfred Leisure Centre
Q. Hove County Cricket Ground
R. St Anne's Wells Gardens
S. West Pier
T. Churchill Square Shops
(please see map for locations)

SMALL BATCH
COFFEE CO.

68 Goldstone Villas, Hove BN3 3RU
T: 01273 220 246 www.smallbatchcoffee.co.uk

Hours - Mon-Fri: 6 - 5	Loyalty Card - Yes	Wifi - No
Sat: 7 - 1	Outdoor Seating - Yes	W.C. - No
Sun: Closed	Wheelchair Access - No	Alcohol - No

Machine - La Marzocco Linea	Beans - Small Batch
Grinder - Mazzer Super Jolly	Soya Milk - Yes

Small Batch Coffee Company was established in 2008 with the focus of filling a gap in the UK market for the type of small, family run roasteries that have long since been commonplace in New Zealand and Australia. In the years that have elapsed Small Batch has flourished, becoming one of the main coffee suppliers to the pubs, bars, restaurants and independent cafés of Brighton and Hove.

Their roastery near Hove station incorporates a high-end espresso bar, serving coffee produced from the finest quality Arabica beans that are roasted daily in batches no bigger than 12kg to ensure freshness. Their espresso blend is changed throughout the year in order that it remains seasonal and incorporates the best of the current crops from around the world. Being an independent coffee roasting company also allows Small Batch to work alongside café owners to produce bespoke blends depending on their individual requirements and to provide barista training where it is required.

Like many of the best boutique roasters and coffee shops, Small Batch adhere to a direct trade principle that not only ensures the highest quality product but also serves the ethical purpose of rewarding the farmers and growers fairly for the speciality grade coffee they produce. In turn, this method also allows the supplier to work directly with the coffee farmers to ensure that social, environmental and wildlife conservation issues meet or exceed local requirements. From a customer point of view, whether buying wholesale or a single cup at the café, it gives assurance that your purchase is of the highest standard.

On a weekday the aroma of the freshly roasted coffee beans drifts from the Small Batch doorway, a sign that the coffee you're drinking will have been roasted, tasted and hand blended a matter of hours before it reaches your cup. From the very beginnings of the growing process, through to the beans that are ground in the bars and cafés across the city, Small Batch will have considered all the elements that go into producing the perfect cup of coffee. They have recently opened a second coffee shop at 67B Church Road, Hove – yet another chance to enjoy the fruits of their labour. Further proof, if any were needed, that small, bespoke roasteries like this are having a big impact on the way we think about coffee throughout the UK.

ETHEL'S KITCHEN

59 Blatchington Road, Hove BN3 3YJ
T: 01273 203 204 www.ethelskitchen.co.uk

Hours - Mon-Fri: 8.30 - 5	Loyalty Card - Yes	Wifi - No
Sat: 8.30 - 5	Outdoor Seating - Yes	W.C. - Yes
Sun: 9 - 5	Wheelchair Access - No	Alcohol - No

| Machine - Rancilio Midi CD | Beans - Union Hand-Roasted |
| Grinder - Mazzer Luigi | Soya Milk - Yes |

Named after Grandma Ethel, whose granddaughter owns and manages the café, Ethel's Kitchen merges the essence of her culinary legacy with modern British food, loose leaf teas and speciality grade coffee. Upon entering you are greeted by a fine display of homemade cakes, and the bone china cups and saucers on shelves behind the counter are a nod to the wholesome traditions of afternoon tea. From the front room of Ethel's Kitchen a small flight of stairs lead down to another seating area where the exposed floorboards, antique furniture and display dishes adorning the walls are a continuum of the relaxed, rustic decoration throughout the café.

Their coffee is sourced by Union Hand-Roasted who apply a similar diligence to producing high quality, ethical coffee as Ethel's Kitchen do in realising the spirit of British home cooking. On the menu, staple favourites like eggy bread, homemade soups, jacket potatoes and traditional Sunday roasts are given a modern twist, with every meal made from scratch using mostly organic produce. In short, it's all healthy, hearty, homely fare. Grandma would be proud.

TREACLE & CO

164 Church Road, Hove BN3 2DL
T: 01273 933 695 www.treacleandco.co.uk

Hours - Mon-Fri: 8.30-5.30	Loyalty Card - Yes	Wifi - Yes
Sat: 9 - 5.30	Outdoor Seating - Yes	W.C. - Yes
Sun: 12 - 5	Wheelchair Access - Yes	Alcohol - No

Machine - Nuova Simonelli Aurelia	Beans - Monmouth
Grinder - Anfim Milano	Soya Milk - Yes

With a decade of experience as a pâtisserie chef behind her, Melody Razak established Treacle & Co. in 2007 with a view to supplying her wares to the sweet toothed inhabitants of Brighton & Hove. Her selection of handmade cakes, biscuits and brownies are made the old fashioned way with only the best local, free range and organic ingredients. Working within the confines of her home kitchen, the business grew to the point where the space, and indeed her neighbours, could no longer cope with the increasing burden of the late night baking sessions and the popularity of her finished creations. Thankfully, in July 2010, the Treacle & Co. HQ was relocated to a much more convenient home on Church Road, complete with original 1930s era tiling. Along with all the home-baked delicacies for which the company is renowned, the café also serves up Monmouth Coffee Company's organic espresso blend and tea courtesy of Kemptown's Metrodeco. Throw into the mix a selection of vintage school chairs and tables, a window display featuring genuine Canadian moose antlers and a jumble of antique mirrors and home wares and you have the quirkiest new café in town.

I GIGI CAFÉ

31a Western Road, Hove BN3 1AF
T: 01273 775 257 www.igigigeneralstore.com

Hours - Mon-Fri: 10 - 5	Loyalty Card - No	Wifi - Yes
Sat: 10 - 5	Outdoor Seating - No	W.C. - Yes
Sun: 11 - 5	Wheelchair Access - No	Alcohol - No

Machine - Rancillio Classe 6	Beans - Monmouth
Grinder - Ceado	Soya Milk - Yes

One of the many simple pleasures to be had in Brighton & Hove is finding the cafés that are tucked away or hidden from view, those places that are stumbled upon and end up exceeding all expectations.

Housed on the first floor of their General Store, the beautifully presented i gigi café most definitely falls into this category. The antique spiral staircase on the ground floor leads up into the bright, one room kitchen-café where the rustic furniture is bathed in light from the expansive, single-paned front window that overlooks the bustle of Western Road. The space is tastefully decorated in shades of cream and white and the understated elegance of the space makes for a relaxed atmosphere. The food on offer at i gigi is as homely and wholesome as the décor, and their lunch boards, Welsh rarebit and delicious homemade cakes - displayed beneath traditional bell jar cake stands - are famed amongst those in the know. i gigi also serves Brazilian blend Monmouth coffee and a selection of Tea Pigs whole leaf teas making it a perfect spot for breakfast, brunch, lunch, or just a well deserved caffeine break. It's all just waiting to be discovered.

BLACK GOLD
FOUNDATION

FIND OUT WHAT YOU CAN DO

AT

WWW.BLACKGOLDFOUNDATION.ORG

The Black Gold Foundation is committed to creating systemic change in the global coffee industry. The Foundation was established in response to the impact of the award-winning film "Black Gold".

roasted

From beans to baristas

We are a local independent coffee distributor dedicated to supplying the coffee loving community of Sussex exceptional quality coffee machines, products and services. All of our coffee is freshly roasted to order and we manage our stock diligently to ensure fresh, flavourful coffee that exceeds even the most demanding coffee connoisseur's expectations.

Our passion for coffee goes beyond simply selling great stuff. We work with some of the city's finest baristas to offer a range of barista training services at roasted's barista school and tasting room. This unique program ensures that our customers have both the equipment and the knowledge they need to create the perfect cup of coffee with every shot. Remember, we love coffee, you love coffee.

Give us a call or check out our website to learn more about what makes roasted different.

30 – 31 Devonshire Place, Brighton, East Sussex, BN2 1QB
t: 0845 017 6661 e: thirsty@roasted.co.uk w: roasted.co.uk

BEST OF THE REST

Other independent cafés worth visiting in Brighton & Hove

NORTH LAINE

COCOA
48 Queen's Road, Brighton BN1 3XB
T: 01273 777 412
www.cocoabrighton.co.uk

NIA
87-88 Trafalgar Street, Brighton BN1 4ER
T: 01273 671 371
www.nia-brighton.co.uk

MOKSHA CAFFÈ
4-5 York Place, Brighton BN1 4GU
T: 01273 248 890
www.mokshacaffe.com

ROCK OLA
29 Tidy Street, Brighton BN1 4EL
T: 01273 673 744

SEASONS CAFÈ
36 Gloucester Road, Brighton BN1 4AQ
T: 01273 689 388
www.seasonscafe.co.uk

INSIDE OUT CAFÉ
95 Gloucester Road, Brighton BN1 4AP
T: 01273 692 912

THE DUMB WAITER
28 Sydney Street, Brighton BN1 4EP
T: 01273 602 526

OFF BEAT COFFEE BAR
37 Sydney Street, Brighton BN1 4EP
T: 01273 604 206

KENSINGTON CAFÉ
1 Kensington Gardens, Brighton BN1 4AL
T: 01273 570 963

BRIGHTON COFFEE CO.
35 Kensington Gardens, Brighton BN1 4AL
T: 01273 690 643
www.brightoncoffee.co.uk

IYDEA
17 Kensington Gardens, Brighton BN1 4AL
T: 01273 667 992
web.mac.com/iydea

CAFÉ DELICE
40 Kensington Gardens, Brighton BN1 4AL
T: 01273 622 519
www.cafedelice.co.uk

INFINITY FOODS CAFÉ
50 Gardner Street, Brighton BN1 1UN
T: 01273 670 743
www.infinityfoods.co.uk

TEMPTATION
56 Gardner Street, Brighton BN1 1UN
T: 01273 673 045
www.brightontemptation.com

CAPERS
27 Gardner Street, Brighton BN1 1UP
T: 01273 675 550
www.capers-brighton.com

LA GIGO GI
24 New Road, Brighton BN1 1UF
T: 01273 687 753

PAVILION GARDENS CAFÉ
Royal Pavilion Gardens, Brighton BN1 1UG
T: 01273 730 712
www.paviliongardenscafe.co.uk

TEA COSY
3 George Street, Brighton BN2 1RH
www.theteacosy.co.uk

METRODECO & MDTEA
38 Upper St. James's Street, Brighton BN2 1JN
T: 07956 978 115
www.metro-deco.com

THE BOOKROOM CAFÉ
91 St. Georges Road, Brighton BN2 1EE
T: 01273 682 110
www.kemptownbookshop.co.uk

KEMPTOWN TRADING POST & CAFÉ
28 St. Georges Road, Brighton BN2 1ED
T: 01273 698 873
www.kemptowntradingpost.co.uk

SPINELLI COFFEE
24 Garnet House, College Road, Brighton, BN2 1JB
T: 01273 818 819
&
111 St. James's Street Brighton, BN2 1TH
T: 01273 818 084   www.spinellicoffee.co.uk

THE LANES

NAKED TEA & COFFEE COMPANY
3 Meeting House Lane, Brighton BN1 1HB
T: 01273 326 080

CHOCCYWOCCYDOODAH
27 Middle Street, Brighton BN1 1AL
T: 01273 732 232
www.choccywoccydoodah.com

MOCK TURTLE TEA SHOP
4 Pool Valley, Brighton BN1 1NJ
T: 01273 327 380

WEST BRIGHTON & HOVE

BEACH HOUSE CAFÉ
21 Kings Road Arches, Brighton BN1 2LN
T: 08721 486 446

KOBA CAFÉ
135 Western Road, Brighton BN3 4FF
T: 01273 720 059

FOODEE...LICIOUS
75-76 Western Road, Hove BN3 2JQ
T: 01273 727 909
www.foodee-licious.com

LA FOURCHETTE PÂTISSERIE
42 Church Road, Hove BN3 2FN
T: 01273 722 556
www.lafourchette.co.uk

9BAR
118 Church Road, Hove BN3 2EA
T: 01273 721 838
www.9bar.co.uk

MARROCCOS
8 King's Esplanade, Hove BN3 2WA
T: 01273 203 764
www.marroccos-restaurant.co.uk

CAFFÈ BAR ITALIA DI NAPOLI
24 George Street, Hove BN3 3YB

HOVE PARK CAFÉ
Hove Park, Hove BN3 7BF
T: 01273 727 003

DRURY TEA & COFFEE
12-16 Richardson Road, Hove BN3 5RB
T: 01273 888 600
www.drurysouthern.co.uk

Women in a Coffee Kids-supported organic gardening project in Oaxaca, Mexico, show off the fruits of their labor.

COFFEE KIDS·

Sustainable, high-quality coffee can only come from sustainable, healthy communities. For the past 23 years, Coffee Kids has brought change to coffee-producing communities.

Help us bring prosperity full circle.

www.coffeekids.org

Coffee Kids works with coffee-farming families to improve their lives and livelihoods.

Coffee Kids fosters sustainability in coffee-growing communities by working in the following areas:

Education
Health Awareness
Economic Diversification
Food Security
Capacity Building

To learn more about Coffee Kids or to make a donation, please visit **www.coffeekids.org/uk** or email **info-uk@coffeekids.org**

COFFEE GLOSSARY

A list of terms often used within the coffee industry.

ACIDITY
One of the three principal tastes employed by professional coffee tasters in detailing a particular coffee or blend. When used in coffee terms acidity is a desirable characteristic, providing a bright, vibrant quality.

AMERICANO
(*Caffè Americano*)
A term coined during World War II when American GIs stationed in Europe would add hot water to their espresso to replicate the coffee they were accustomed to drinking in the United States. Essentially the term still means an espresso with added hot water.

ARABICA (*Coffea Arabica*)
The most widely grown species of coffee tree, Arabica accounts for approximately 70% of the world's coffee and thrives when grown at high elevation in cooler and dryer climates. It is generally seen as superior in terms of taste and quality to other coffee species. The plant was originally indigenous to Ethiopia but the name Arabica is derived from the Arabian Peninsula, having been exported there in large quantities. It is believed to be the first coffee species to be cultivated, with evidence of its growth dating back well over 1000 years.

BARISTA
The Italian term for *bar person* which now connotes a professional espresso machine operator.

BLEND
A combination of two or more coffee subspecies (such as Bourbon or Typica) that are blended together. It can lead to a more balanced coffee flavour or flavours that are greater than the sum total of its parts.

BODY
Describes the heaviness of the coffee on the tongue when tasted (for example thin, watery, oily, thick or syrupy).

BREW TIME
Contact time between water and coffee. The guideline for a correctly brewed espresso is between 20 and 30 seconds, though the exact times are dictated by roasting dates, blend components and many other variables.

CAPPUCCINO
Though there are many variations, the cappuccino is essentially a milky espresso-based drink with more foam than a latte. Its original name was *kapuziner* and dates back to 19th century Vienna.

CORTADO
A traditional Spanish coffee made up of an espresso shot cut with a small amount of steamed milk without much foam. A Spanish piccolo.

CREMA
The golden foam that covers the surface of an espresso shot. Crema is made by the pressurised brew water forcing its way through the coffee bed.

CUPPING
The procedure employed by coffee tasters in order to evaluate samples of coffee beans, the key evaluation characteristics being aroma, acidity, body and flavour.

DOSAGE
The amount of ground coffee used to produce an espresso shot. Typically around 7-11 grams of coffee is used for a single espresso shot and 16-25 grams for a double.

ESPRESSO
The basis of most coffee beverages served in cafés, an espresso shot is produced when hot water is forced at high pressure through a compressed bed of finely ground coffee in an espresso machine. This generally takes between 20 and 30 seconds and yields 20-30 mls of liquid. Much like the English word 'express', the term refers to the speed of its preparation (compared to other coffee brewing methods) and also conveys 'expressly' or 'just for you.'

FLAT WHITE
An espresso based beverage invented in Australia or New Zealand prepared by pouring steamed milk with a thin layer of microfoam over a single or double shot of espresso.

GRIND
Whole coffee beans are ground to different sizes depending on the brew method. As a rule the longer the brew time, the larger or courser the grind. So, the espresso grind is small or fine and takes up to approximately 30 seconds, whereas the cafetiere grind is coarser and is brewed for approximately 4 minutes.

LATTE (*Caffè Latte*)
Literally translated from the Italian for 'coffee and milk', a latte is a single espresso shot combined with foamed milk and is usually served in a glass.

LATTE ART
The creation of a pattern or design on the surface of a coffee beverage by either free pouring steamed milk over an espresso shot or etching designs onto the finished coffee using a coffee stirrer. Common types of latte art are the Rosetta or the heart shape.

LONG BLACK
A double shot of espresso pulled into hot water. The Antipodean version of an Americano.

MACCHIATO (*Caffè Macchiato*)
An espresso "marked" with a small amount of foamed milk, usually about a teaspoon.

MICROFOAM
Steamed milk with small, almost imperceptible bubbles that comprise a basic requirement for pouring.

MICRO-LOT COFFEES
A small lot of coffee that has benefited from conditions, such as soil, shade or selective picking, that has been isolated in one particular area of a farm. These conditions can create a unique character to the coffee which sets it apart from the rest of the crop in terms of quality. Due to the extra preparation required, their resulting quality and the small scale of their production, micro-lot coffees also fetch higher prices.

OVER EXTRACTED
Bitter, harsh and unpleasant flavours that are the result of the contact time between water and coffee grounds being too long or brew water that is too hot.

PICCOLO
Literally meaning 'small' in Italian, a Piccolo is a smaller variant of the latte. Consists of an espresso or ristretto shot, topped with steamed milk and is usually served in a small glass at a 1:1 ratio of espresso to milk.

RISTRETTO
A "restricted" espresso. A ristretto is richer and more intense than a traditional espresso shot due to the smaller volume of brew water in comparison to coffee.

ROAST
The method of heating green coffee beans to approximately 200-220 °C in order to develop desirable flavours.

ROBUSTA (*Coffea Canephora*)
Behind Arabica, Robusta is the other primary coffee species to be used commercially. Unlike Arabica, Robusta has a shallow root system and grows a robust tree or shrub that is less susceptible to pests and disease, requires less care in growing and can flourish at low altitudes. The typical yield of Robusta is twice that of Arabica and the resulting coffee contains twice as much caffeine, though less complex flavours. Robusta is often used as a filler in lower-quality filter blends and instant coffees.

SHOT
A single brewed espresso.

SINGLE-ORIGIN COFFEE
Coffee from one country. Single-origin coffees can capture the essence of a particular country due to variants such as soil, altitude and climate specific to that growing area. Within single origin definitions there are also single estate coffees, which refers to an area or estate within that country of origin, akin to wine regions.

TAMP/TAMPING

The method by which loose coffee grounds are compressed and compacted into a portafilter basket in preparation for brewing espresso.

TAMPER

The device used for tamping or compacting coffee grounds.

UNDER EXTRACTED

When contact time, temperature or turbulence is insufficient to fully extract desirable flavours from coffee.

WHOLE BEAN COFFEE

Coffee beans that have been roasted but have yet to be ground.

Many thanks to Andrew Tolley for his help and expertise in compiling this list.

Coffea arabica

THANKS

Andrew, Selina, Veronica, Chloe & Fergus @ **Taylor St.**
Taras, Ame, Adam & Paul @ **Coffee@33**
Vincent, Thierry & Eddie @ **Mange Tout & Plateau**
Harry & Tony @ **Farm**
Chris @ **Cream Tea**
Tim @ **Redroaster**
Rick, Matt & Chloe @ **Ground**
Sean @ **Frankie's Grinder**
Stephane @ **Tic Toc**
Richard, Steve, Ashley, Duné, Jenny & Joseph @ **Marwood**
Alan, Brad, Sascha, Tony & Gilda @ **Small Batch**
Alex & Emma @ **i gigi**
Glenda, Sarah-Louise & George @ **Ethel's Kitchen**
Melody & Alyssa @ **Treacle & Co.**
James & Mark @ **Café Coho**
Rob & Sinclair @ **Redwood**

Also a big thanks to Mr. Smith at the Workshop, B.P. Evans,
Susan & Robin Sykes, Jackie and Victor, Meg, Rachael, Cal,
Matt Barker, Marc and Arash, Harry Bohay-Nowell, Eleonora
D'Ambrosio, Stephane Vincent, James Dean White, Dominic
at Four Corners Print, Marc Francis, Elisa Kelly, Richard & Andy
at Roasted, Alan Cunliffe, Chris Logan, Anton & John and to
Brighton & Hove City Council.